GETTING BETTER

Marie McNamara

Gate
HOUSE

Getting Better
Text copyright © Marie McNamara 2006
Illustrations copyright © Ian Bobb 2007
Edited by Catherine White

First published and distributed in 2007 by Gatehouse Media Limited
Reprinted in 2017

ISBN: 978-1-84231-026-7

British Library Cataloguing-in-Publication Data:
A catalogue record for this book is available from the British Library

Gatehouse Media Limited provides an opportunity for writers to express their thoughts and feelings on aspects of their lives. The views expressed are not necessarily those of the publishers.

Author's Note

Thank you to everyone who let me down – they made me stronger - and to everyone who's been there for me.

On my own with a teenager
and two small children.
Sat at home,
living off benefits.
I hated it!
I wanted so much more
for me and for my children.

A drive to the seaside was my escape.
St. Annes is a beautiful place.
I just used to get up,
put the children in the car and go.
When I was there,
I could forget about where I lived.
I would watch the kids
building sandcastles on the beach.
Then we would get some dinner
from the chippy.

Afterwards the kids would paddle
in the boating pool.
All the other mums, dads,
grandmas and grandpas sat around,
eating ice cream
and watching their children.
My kids loved it.
I'd get a lump in my throat
just watching them having fun.
I never wanted to go home.

I didn't plan to go back to education.
The lone parent advisor at the job centre
signed me up for a computer course.
But I couldn't read and write very well.
I could not spell at all.

Bill, my teacher, had to read and explain
what it said on the computer screen.
He had to spell words for me.
His patience and kindness
helped me through.
He encouraged me to carry on.
He said, "I've got to hand it to you.
You always come back."

Before, I could never fill in forms.
They may as well have been written
in another language.
In the end, I didn't even look at them.
I asked my sister to fill them in for me
and I just signed them.
Now, I was beginning
to fill in forms on my own.

I began to help my children
with their homework -
something I could never do before.
As I improved,
so did their results at school.

Going back to education
was changing all our lives.
History was not going to repeat itself.
I was making sure of that.

I took another course
called Access to Health and Nursing.
I realised I wanted to be a nurse,
but I needed more qualifications.

I filled out all the forms myself
to apply to study nursing
... at university!

Vicky, my English teacher,
put my name forward
for a NIACE award.
I won it.
I couldn't believe it.
I'd never won anything before.

Then, a year later,
I won a Helena Kennedy
Foundation Award,
for adult learners
who have overcome barriers
to continue with their education.

We went to London,
had tea at the House of Lords
and Baroness Helena Kennedy QC
presented me with the award.

Returning to education
to learn to read and write,
was one of the most frightening things
I have done,
but it was also one of the best.

Sometimes, I found it too hard
and cried.

Sometimes, I wanted to quit.

My beautiful children
gave me the will to keep going.
My teachers gave me strength.
They told me that,
with hard work,
I could make it.

I wanted to be independent.

I wanted to feel pride.

I wanted to give my children
a better chance.

Now our lives are getting better.

About the Author

I split up from the kids' dad because of his addiction to drugs. Everyone knew what he was getting up to – his family, some of my family, my friends - everyone except me. No one had the decency to tell me. It made me hate the estate we lived on. I was angry most of the time and when I wasn't angry, I was sad. Everything I did felt like an effort. I just wanted to sit down and never get up again. My heart would beat really loud and I always felt sick. I'd sit and look at my children and get pains in my chest, hardly able to breathe at the thought of them having only me to rely on. ME! This mess that was always shouting and crying.

Going to the seaside was an escape for me. Everything seemed so nice. Then, almost by chance, I ended up back in education. I learned to read, write and spell. It has been a long journey with many highs and lows. I'm not quite there yet but life is getting better, for me and for my children.

After three years back in education, Marie was accepted to University where she is now studying to become a nurse.

"I look back sometimes and I can't believe how much my life has changed. Hopefully, in three years, I will be able to return to work, doing a job of my own choice and, at the same time, be able to support my children - all because I learned to read, write and spell."

Gatehouse Books®

Our writers are adults who are developing their basic reading and writing skills. Their ideas and experiences make fascinating material for any reader, but are particularly relevant for adults working on their own reading and writing skills. The writing often strikes a chord with the reader - a shared experience of struggling against many odds.

The format of our books is clear and uncluttered. The language is familiar and the text is often line-broken, so that each line ends at a natural pause.

Gatehouse Books are widely used within Adult Basic Education throughout the English speaking world. They are also a valuable resource within the Prison Education Service and Probation Services, Social Services and secondary schools.

Catalogue available

Gatehouse Media Limited
PO Box 965
Warrington
WA4 9DE

Tel: 01925 267778
Website: www.gatehousebooks.com
E-mail: info@gatehousebooks.com

If you have enjoyed this book, why not try one of these titles from the Gatehouse Books series:

Secrets ISBN: 978-1-84231-24-3
by Sue Torr MBE

Sue was a dinner lady when, at the age of 38, she finally faced up to the fact that she couldn't read or write. This is an autobiographical account of Sue's life without literacy. The book is designed for both beginner readers and more confident readers, with a standard text on the left-hand page and a simplified text on the facing page.

Don't Give Up ISBN: 978-1-84231-020-5
by Mavis Beharrie

Mavis is determined to pass her driving test in spite of her dyslexia. This story has a positive and inspiring message for the reader.

Not So Bothered ISBN: 978-1-84231-021-2
by Eric Newsham

A day out ends in disaster. Eric gives us a vivid and amusing account of his eventful journey home.

Bob's Problem ISBN: 978-1-84231-056-4
by Margaret Adams

Bob likes his job on the dairy counter at Asco supermarket, but his boss has other plans for him. Bob is forced to reveal his problem. Then one day, a shocking event puts Bob's life on the line.